In Love With Single

In Love With Single
Copyright © 2019 by Alisia Latoi
All rights reserved.

This is a work of fiction. Names, characters, places and incidents either are the product of the authors' imagination or are used fictitiously, and any resemblance to any actual persons, living or dead, events, or locales is entirely coincidental.

No part of this book may be reproduced or transmitted in any form or by any means, electronic or mechanical, including photocopying, recording, or by any information storage and retrieval system, without permission in writing from the copyright owner.

Published by GoPublish, an imprint of Visual Adjectives, Delray Beach, Florida.

GoPublish
14280 Military Trail, #7501
Delray Beach, Florida 33482

Web: www.GoPublishYourBook.com
Email: info@GoPublishYourBook.com

ISBN-13: 978-1-941901-39-7
Paperback Edition November 2019

Dedicated to all the ears that listened to me vent until I was prepared to write.

In Love With Single
by Alisia Latoi

Table of Contents

Open Mic 14
Tallest Tree 16
Socially Awkward 18
No Attention 20
My Solo Walk 22
Applaud Regret 24
Relevance of Age 26
To Welcome 35 28
Innocent One 30
Be Similar 32
You are the One 34

Interview Drag 38
Working Two 42
Stating the Obvious 44
They and You 46
Selfie 48
Semi 50
Chit-Chat 52
The Moon and Constellation 54
Appreciation for the Anticipation 56
Distant Family 58
Prodigal 62
Simple 64
Some Still Sit 66

Good Poems 70
Braces on Brokenness 72
Carry My Tears 74
Ripples 78
Great Again 80
Trending 82
I Favored Kindness 84
It Happen to Whom 86

Table of Contents

A Victim's Legend 88
Not A Fan 90
Not A Fan 90

Hollow 96
Connecting Parts 98
That Day 100
Perfect Apron 102
I Observed a Wife 104
The Silence Meaning Thru 106
Repeat Break 108
Let's Try This Again 110

As If 116
Someone Already Has You 118
90's Babe 120
Twist My Hair 122
Mind Song 124
Pump 9 126
Heard Nothing 128
Triggers 130
Confidently Insecure 132
One-sided View 134
No X's 136
Purchased Vibration 140

Without A Pair 146
For Three Words 148
Be Direct 150
Single Status? 152
Never Lowered 154
Amends To Body 156
In Love with Single 158

Alisia Latoi

"Good evening Ms. Latoi. My name is Harriet Fields. I'll be conducting your interview for the Balance magazine article. I know this will be your first feature as an author. Are you ready?" The journalist asked this with an anticipated smile as we set in the living room I'd meticulously prepared for this evening. The two glasses of water, no ice, and plain décor provided no distractions. Yet, I still weighed in the present with many memories. One of such asked the same question of me at the age of naivety.

Aren't you glad your parents are away? Before you go to sleep we're going to play a little game, okay. You don't have to do anything but lay in bed. I'm going touch you and place your hands where it is I want you to touch me. It may feel weird but you can't say anything or you'll lose.

Are you ready?

"Yes, I'm ready," I replied. Snapping back into the current, I mimicked her anticipated smile.
"Great, before we began I'd like to briefly run through the questions I'll be asking", she continued. I nodded my head, prompting her to go on, although my mind sustained to recollect.

Mom, something happened to me a long time ago and it's caused me to feel depressed at times. Well, she replied, you need to go to church and take all things to God in prayer.

In Love With Single

Such flashbacks took me through forgiven events though having left residue. While others have caused me to proceed in doing everything with caution having only complete confidence in the situations I have control over.

"Amen pastor," the congregation resounded in response to his declaration. I'm speaking to the single men and women of the church. You have to be specific in your prayers. Don't just ask God to send you someone. Be detailed with your declaration as to the attributes you are looking for in a significant other and God will provide.

(That night)

Dear God,
I want a man with the below qualities and physical appearance.

However, most of my experiences have shaped me in to the person sitting here today, prepared for this interview.

"Nice of you to join us high school graduates. Now let me ask you the same question you asked me", my best friend announced, "what do you want your life to look like ten years from now?"

"I'll probably end up taking on the teaching profession", I replied skeptically, "but I hope to be married, settled, and financially secure by then."

With the sound of Ms. Field's gulp of water, I was brought temporarily back to the present when she asked, "Out of those, are there any questions you would like me to avoid?"

"Why'd you agree to come over here", he asked?

"Well, I thought you just wanted to talk; get to know each other better", I replied.

"What, are you a virgin?"

In annoyance I said, "Well, kinda."

"You're too old for that shit", he shouted, "you know what; just leave".

"Sex", I voiced to the journalist ardently. I want to avoid all the questions related to my sexual experience. My book provides detail enough. With that the journalist laughed in acknowledgment of my request and pressed record.

Alisia Latoi

Introverted

Synonyms: shy, reserved, withdrawn, reticent, diffident, retiring, quiet; introspective, introvert, inward-looking, self-absorbed; pensive, contemplative, thoughtful, meditative, reflective

In Love With Single

"Welcome listeners and readers," Ms. Fields began. "Today I have the pleasure of speaking with an on the rise poet and author, Alisia Latoi."

Journalist:

In your debut book, "Going Through Phases", you mentioned that feelings of discomfort when faced with human interactions drew you to write. Could you dive deeper and explain what it is about the craft that makes, specifically poetry, your resolve?

Author:

I use to hold certain things heavy within my heart in which I couldn't bring myself to express verbally or provide detail. In that era, I found it easiest to write ambiguously, in the form of poetry as a means of release. It became cathartic. Today, while I have less trouble communicating, I still continue to express an array of emotions, experiences, and sentiments through the writing form.

Open Mic

In Love With Single

I wrote the lyrics but am incapable of reciting them verbatim;

So, I plan to hold this phone, possibly my book, look down, and read to you;

I may lack the passionate expression expected of spoken word;

Yet, my approach aspires to be authentic;

You don't have to relate to my lyrics;

But I hope you'll listen;

Well enough to encourage the first move towards the stage of vulnerability;

Wishing you not receive me winter cold;

Neither view me an opposing flow;

I implore the witness to welcome springs aura;

As I experiment with this open mic;

By placing myself standing in front;

With being surprisingly not discomforted;

I spoke my poetry to strangers.

Tallest Tree

In Love With Single

Little girl saw the tree for the first time;

Standing dominantly tallest in a field of greens.

Initially intimidated by its appearance;

The tree made itself familiar by association;

Becoming a friend considered family.

Little girl climbed up as it welcomed her;

Often suggesting she do;

When no one else was around.

She sat on the trees sturdy branch;

As its leaves felt her privately;

In a place where only those who birth her had seen.

She lost comfort in the tallest tree.

Flinching unknowingly;

Familiarity doesn't welcome touch.

Age grew a voice;

But back in the forest,

Little girl walked quietly;

Prematurely she experienced too much.

Socially Awkward

In Love With Single

You probably walked away

Thinking it would've been best to avoid this person

While reflecting on the uneasiness of my flow;

Maybe it would provide you comfort to know

That I would sometimes prefer it if people didn't talk to me;

Spare me a scene of social awkwardness

By ignoring the urge to attempt interaction;

Perhaps I should have warned you before your utterance

That my words drag in comparison to my thoughts

And my nervous ways mask the calmness of my heart;

Setting aside what causes the difficulty

In truth, I wanted someone to connect with;

Among a crowd

It's always nice to be seen and have your whispers heard;

So, smiling came with ease

As I watched your footsteps move towards me

I attempted to silence my social inabilities and interact naturally

But my long pauses and awkward mannerisms caused the participator uneasiness

Then the doorbell rang to welcome new faces;

And from me

You walked away.

No Attention

In Love With Single

Boldness flies on weightless wings
Carrying fears, I don't want seen
Propelling me to acknowledge
The small voice ignored
That answers the question
To my solar eclipse
Which causes a speedy heart
In a crowd of others
To hide and deflect
The attention away from me
So that I could remain
In the background
Where I'm most comfortable being,
Not hinting on insecurities,
Confidence guides my flight,
Nonetheless, in a direction
That leads me far from
The spotlight.

My Solo Walk

In Love With Single

One leg lifts the anxious foot
That is ready to feel the sand.
A familiar sensation
The other foot is excited to share.
As soon as one foot makes contact
The other releases.
Both feet meet common ground
When movement ceases.
They point towards the direction of the sunrise
And watch the waves propel closer to the toes.
Reveling in the noise the water makes.
Crashing in to the land with such force.
Reshaping each grain around my imprint
Until one leg lifts again,
Revealing my longing foot,
Then it drops and the other one lifts.
Missing the unified contact,
My head turns,
Signaling my eyes to look back
To witness the water glide over my footprints
Causing them to disappear.

Applaud Regret

In Love With Single

The last time I had a night like this,
My place of prostrate comfort didn't offer solace,
In that moonlit moment nothing else existed,
But the desire to shut my eyes until the next morning,
Still thoughts void of purpose continued to flow,
As I tussled in hopes of finding relaxation,
Insomnia's grip never weakened.
Making tonight familiar,
As the sleep won't come despite the attempt,
Thoughts arrive while awake fighting restlessness,
In this moment there isn't anything else but acceptance.
I toss to find bits of remorse,
I turn to find pieces of disappointment,
I can't exclude myself from,
A life existing with no regrets,
I applaud each of them,
The welcome makes it easier
To weaken insomnia's hold,
By remaining open to the unsmooth path
That struggles to keep peace close.

Relevance of Age

In Love With Single

Age doesn't become relevant
Until I think about kids.
It's the next most question asked of me
Besides why I walk single.
There is no readiness for parenthood.
No longer a need for two.
Just a matter of deciding which avenue.
Sometimes I lean towards having none
When I focus on the world's disgrace.
To born the pure,
Watch the innocence grow,
Hopefully raise him or her to not fit the mold of chaos,
Pray that nothing strikes their life,
Most assuredly not before my own.
Do I want a child?
Periodically, I remain unsure.
I weigh my options;
Foster, adoption, artificial insemination, or wait for the one.
Making my age relevant again.
I have enough love to give.
A child will call me mother,
I sense it in my future,
The day and avenue,
I'll discover.

To Welcome 35

In Love With Single

If my looks don't reveal the truthful age;

I am pleased.

If, opposingly, my looks add on years;

I am still pleased.

With having not placed my trust in perceptions voice,

The little girl that was me would be proud of the woman succeeding.

Having feed off of the wisdom that comes with each passing day,

Life is full of joy and it's full of pain,

Keeping balanced the lever of pride and humility.

I've gained another 8,760 hours in this present.

With that realization, perhaps moments of displeasure will be less.

However, I don't know the number on the scale that displays the weight of impending days.

But this one wish has come to be; I am optimistic that it'll continue as such.

My health, body, and soul remain intact

To welcome 35.

Blowing out the candles,

Taking roughly 20 breaths every 60 seconds while in a resting state,

I beseech the excitement of each minute to take me gracefully to the next age.

Innocent One

In Love With Single

My face is a betrayal,
If you believe your first impression,
Trust in your perception,
Telling you what I am incapable of.
The audience looking at me;
You never witnessed a foul word take formation upon these lips,
Compelling you to ask for forgiveness when in my presence
If profanity leaves yours,
Because my ears seem naïve.
The man with too much history;
You are at fault before a jury,
That's why you don't want to take things with me seriously,
Commit and possibly reconfigure this heart,
Become liable for changing the colors to my painting,
Because my eyes appear too trusting for guilt's exposure.
However, my face deceives.
Although my steps are different,
The walk isn't blameless.
Rebelling against goodness,
Occasionally, strolling on grey pavements,
By demonstrating wild behavior.
Don't be shocked if at times my halo seems removed,
Causing my actions and utterance to baffle you.
I never confessed myself purest among us.
Remember, it is you
Who saw me as
The innocent one.

Be Similar

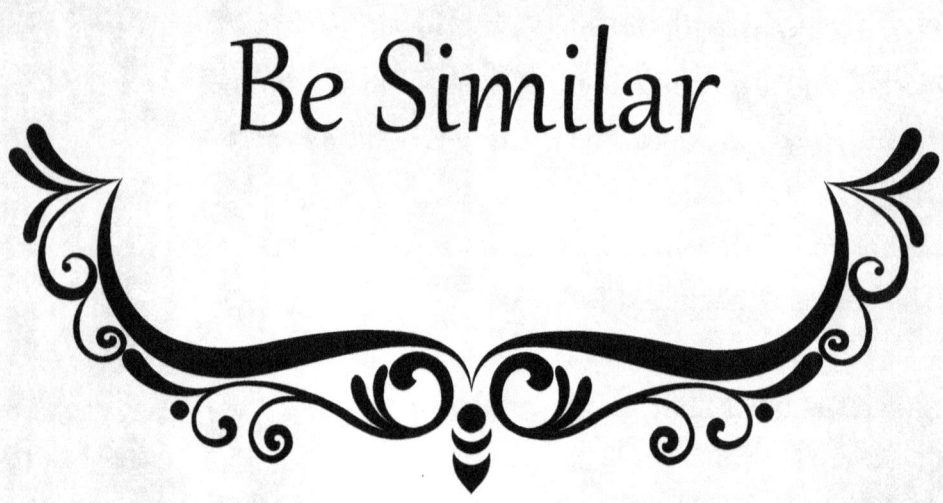

In Love With Single

With eyes.
I saw my skin.
It was darker than yours.
You viewed mine different and yours superior.
In order to be similar,
I bleached it.

With a lighter complexion.
I saw my hair.
It didn't move like yours.
You viewed mine different and yours superior.
In order to be similar,
I covered my natural.

Adorning a wig.
I saw your clothes.
I viewed mine different and yours superior.
In order to be similar,
I shopped at your store.

Wearing high fashion.
I now saw the envy from those unique.
I was no longer viewed as different
But among the superior.
In order to remain similar,
I continued to conform
And lost what use to be
My individuality.

You are the One

In Love With Single

Dear Self,

    You may be looking in the mirror right now. Tempted to spot and acknowledge flaws. But don't just yet. Especially, if you feel they make you inferior. First, wash your face and body, then look again, and instead, state positive affirmations. Stare at yourself intensely because you are at the rate of admiring. Notice the entirety of your body, gestures in your expressions, while taking in your essence. Breathe agelessly but embrace the signs of it on your skin. While doing your hair, remember the mistakes from yesterday and carry imperfections better today. When you fall, rise, and just keep going. See your humanity because it is flawed. Now, acknowledge each of them. Inadequacies are a part of your beauty. As you dress in front of the mirror, secure that calm confidence and put it to work. While you do this, evade self-loathing and self-pity. Only envy if it encourages success. When deciding to put on makeup, know that it's there to enhance not conceal. Lastly, take one final look in the mirror before you tackle the rest of your day. Remember to choose yourself, accept what life gives, and fight for your wants. After nodding your head in approval of the complete look, step out the door knowing you are worth enough for the universe. Walk wearing a veil of assurance in this destined life partner because you are the one for self.

In Love With Single

Journalist:
If you could tell your younger writing-self anything, what would it be?

Author:
I'd tell her that while your tears do get denser and your emotions more complex, your joy becomes lasting and your loneliness is brief.
(Grinning)
I would also tell her to disregard all nay-sayers; you're doing just fine.

Interview Drag

In Love With Single

It is deadly quiet in this lobby as I wait to be seated before a panel of poker-faces for an interview.

I feel ready.

Forgetting my usual failure in and annoyance with the act.

I tend to misplace knowledge and tell fables that boost.

Not intentionally, but some inquiries are ridiculous.

Forcing a made-up answer in avoidance of none at all.

A friend who is an employee here told me of the job.

Which means I may get it despite a lack of field experience.

The job mostly deals with numbers but with training I'll be excellent.

Even though I currently hold a position that mostly consist of filing paper documents.

A task that conceals my poor grades in mathematics.

I'm brought into a conference room, clothed in anxiety and confidence before the presence of three.

"So, tell us a little about yourself."

"Well, I have two degrees."

But the resume in front of them details that.

"I'm a hard worker, who takes good notes, and can catch on quick."

I seem to have overlooked my broad vocabulary.

"Talk about an instance where you exceeded the duties associated with your current position. Tell us about a time you were given a project with little guidance. How did you go about completing the task? What programs did you use?"

Expound.

"I'm one of the top producers on my team, offering suggestions that come in to fruition. I worked in programs with little to no training, yet, I am proficient in all my current duties."

Embellishment.

"Talk about a time you were given a tedious task related to the work you may partake in at this company. One in which you created an action plan that made the assignment more efficient."

Provide detail.

"Recently, I created a system of logging in data that tracks the fluctuation of revenue received within the department."

Complete lie.

"Do you have any questions for us?"

"None at this time."

In Love With Single

"Is there anything you'd like to add before we conclude?"

"I just want you to know that I'm a hard worker, who takes good notes, and can catch on quick."

Why am I repeating this?

"One last inquiry. Are you bilingual?"

It was on the job description as a requirement, however, the position entails mostly numbers.

I don't believe knowing another language is indeed necessary.

"No."

But if hired at the high salary offered, I could be in weeks.

"Thank you for your time."

"Thank you. I hope to hear from you soon."

It was a celebration in my car as I played the most hyped song on my playlist.

When my phone pinged with an email, I half expected it to be another job contacting me for an interview.

However, this transcript read,

"Thank you for your interest in our company. After further review of your experience and interview responses, the company has decided to proceed with other candidates."

Working Two

In Love With Single

Can I borrow one of your kids, it's income tax time;
Claim them for extra money even though they're not mine.
Maybe I'll marry the next guy to propose;
Love can come later with the money he earns;
A combined annual income worth enough to approve
A loan I wouldn't receive given my own salary;
Nearly impossible to find an apartment that my solo pockets can afford;
Forcing me to seek a roommate I'd want to evict eventually.
She had some extra food stamps and sold them to me.
How she went about obtaining them given our shared circumstance,
Is through an avenue of lies I'm not brave enough to use.
That day, while on my way to the market, a car hit me from behind.
I left the scene.
Thinking, no matter how deep the dent,
A raised premium and high deductible
Made the accident not worth the hassle.
Later, I stood in line at the store overhearing the cashier express
How she holds three jobs.
I tried working two over the holidays,
But I quit one before the term was finished.
A lack of will for working many.
Multiple paychecks may mean the difference between
Owning and renting.
I went home to search for a second income;
Told my roommate she'll need to move out soon;
I'm going to find some extra funds;
Taxes and insurance take much of my income;
Making it seem as though there's little financial benefit when you're on your own.
Single with no dependents.
I'll work more than one till a season is through.
Then place blame, vent, and rant
How the government got me set up to lose.

Stating the Obvious

In Love With Single

Don't you hate when people state the obvious,
Prompting you to respond sarcastically,
Act as though completely oblivious,
While underlyingly annoyed,
And say, "No shit."
I get that it's hard to resist commenting on phrases with direct intent,
However, some statements need no remark,
Some actions don't require descriptions voiced by the doer or observer,
As though those surrounding aren't sensible.
I understand you're compelled to tell me what I already know,
And think it's funny.
Then when I don't join in the hilarity,
But, instead, remark snidely,
You proceed with indignation.
So, allow me to present reality.
If given the opportunity to state what's evident,
Be open to receive,
Because I may be underlyingly annoyed,
Say, "No shit,"
And then provide retorts that cause offense.

They and You

In Love With Single

I've been watching you through a critical lens,
The little chip in your tooth,
The way you sit while everyone stands.

They reveal their skin,
You cover your legs.
They twerk down low,
Your ass stays still but your shoulders dance.
They bond over a guy's foolish ways, exchanging stories,
While you contribute nothing except the nod of your head.
They've tried and done it all,
You keep private your boring life including your risky experiences.
There's are big,
Yours are small.
You get tipsy off of one,
They frown at the limit to the things you've done.
They fit the mold and stay on rhythm with each wave,
Your demeanor remains off beat missing the memo pop culture gave.
They improve contrast to an odd shade,
You add balance to a wild one's gaze.
They wonder about you standing flat in a picture of pumps,
You defend your attendance.
They are accused of bringing the church girl out to party.
You declare the occasional rave is common to every story.
They ask if you're a bad girl?
You say, "No, just in between."
They seem at ease.
You seem tense, so I tease.

I've viewed you critically through a reflective lens,
I even noticed the moment you recognized the difference.
In a scene outside of your average show,
Appearing timid until that moment you bid them goodbye and go home.

Selfie

In Love With Single

I used her as a cover up;
Her big personality hid my wounds from a crowd of dancing fools.
She joined them;
Holding their phones, snapping pictures, and recording moves;
Pressing delete each time the lens didn't capture her best angles;
She wouldn't hit send until it was decided her look was desirable enough.

She always abides by the rules of the dollhouse;
Cover your blemishes,
Wrap your waste to smooth your sides,
Wear heals to impress at all times,
Keep color on your nails, lips, and above the eyes,
Know your best angles for photos,
Maintain your disguise,
Concern yourself only with the illusion,
And imprint on the most guys.

I used you as a cover up,
But once I heard the rules
I no longer cared about my visible wounds.
My sides are always bumpy,
My stomach sometimes pokes out past the tips of my shoes,
My nails, lips, and eyes are bare,
My lashes,

Sometimes it seems to be none there.
My only concern is to not fall while I dance with little rhythm,
Smiling freely with no thought of imprinting on a guy;
With whom, if settles impressed,
Could approach having no worry of an overnight stay
That concludes with an unmasked surprise.
When I pose with the illusionist
I may look untampered with in photos
While rebelling against the dollhouse,
But a compliant me takes selfies perfectly.

Semi

In Love With Single

We were just semi friends;
A little more than associates;
The relation wasn't lasting;
Since you found the convenience ending;
After parting ways;
I found the communion wasn't wasted;
The semi friendship left an impact;
A wrinkle in the wind;
Making it difficult for the next person;
Whom may attempt to wear the same skin;
I'd then remember the part-time
that tried to convince me they were genuine.

Chit-Chat

In Love With Single

The wind whispers, "Some one's talking about me."
I caught the thought behind the look in your eyes
And it's telling me a story that you're saying,
"See the sista over there; her clothes aren't pressed. Her hair isn't curled.
And I have to tell you what she confessed. I promised her I wouldn't repeat.
But how could anyone come in to the workplace and present themselves with such deceit."
I just continue to walk on by,
Close the door to the outside,
Let the rain drops flow down the blabber's window,
And dissipate.
Maybe it's just paranoia.
Then someone confirmed they heard you,
Speaking unkind words aimed at my back,
While appearing to be at least an ally,
Voicing blessings to my face.
It's a nuisance to walk through a school of gnats.
Don't open your mouth to beckon unwelcomed pest.
A word of caution,
You'll swallow,
And continue to hear gibberish spoken by the gossiper.
I smile fully aware of the noise and shielding its affects.
We're all fifteen years or more past teenagers,
Yet pettiness doesn't respect age, I guess?
I'm not a natural hugger,
Particular of those who caress my back,
Weary of their prints becoming attached like the fat around my belly.
I avoid the loose lips in search for open ears to spill what should be sealed.
I dodge the arrows sent from those who believe themselves to be closer to the gates of Heaven.
Aware of my vulnerability to words that may have me at odds with mercy,
I retreat into a cave of peace,
Escaping any retaliation, I could release.

The Moon and Constellation

In Love With Single

I rejoiced when I heard
She had announced their engagement;
The clapping stars aligned behind;
I am a part, but shift to the side for a time;
One of her stars, but not chosen to form her constellation;
As a light I'm invited to participate in all the pre-events;
However, not a selected bright,
 In planning, I wasn't in the mix.
On the day of wedding bells
Her constellation took formation
Leading the bride to her celebration.
I sat and watched, among others,
Gleaming to my greatest capacity.
Nonetheless, not shinning loud enough to be a bridesmaid.
If not, an emotional person, I would easily understand,
Rationally, I do.
Still, I have a small group of friends
With whom my walls become transparent.
As I watched them dance for wedding bells
I had to leave myself behind
And not be stuck on me this night.
I glued myself to a location in the dark blue sky
Next to the one dressed in white and her ladies in waiting.
When my center flickered dim
Arms reached out to pull me in,
Because it's not hard to feel left out, even among close friends.
The hands that touched where those of the moon and constellation
Pushing me out of my own way
So that I could embrace the luminous rays of the festive occasion.

Appreciation for the Anticipation

In Love With Single

I'd wonder when they'd finally play it;
The song I'd waited the past hour to catch;
I had my cassette ready to record;
Adding to the collection of music my ears delighted to hear;
And there was an appreciation for the anticipation
When I grew up before the new;
A love for the walking and searching
Before easy access made the hunt old school.
I'd wait for the house phone to become available
So, I could talk to my friends on 3-way about some dude.
Catch the bus to a location my parents knew nothing about
All to meet up with some crush I swore to like enough to lie.
Then close out the week, laid prostrate, in the back of a pickup truck
Creating my own melodies while watching the stars,
Wishing I was a part of the magnificent;
And with that there was an appreciation,
When I grew up before the new,
A love for the walking and searching
Before easy access made the hunt old school.
Teenage days brought cell phones my way
I could speak regardless of convenience.
Called the him who brought me smiles at the time,
Back when we'd feel the rebellious excitement of staying up all night.
Ordering take out and traveling to Blockbusters to rent movies.
It was; but we never called it a date.
I had a love for the waiting and hoping
Before expediency brought an end to his pursuit.
I tell the new this when impatience rules their ways,
An ungrateful attitude is the crown that illuminates,
They put forth minimal effort
 Because there aren't many mysteries to uncover,
The answers are all available through a device
That can be held in the hand and fits in their pockets.
Sometimes the apprehensions of life lessen the excitement
But I wish they had an appreciation for the anticipation.
They will when it's them who grew up before the new.
Then they'll recall the love for walking and searching
Before easy access made there hunt old school.

Distant Family

In Love With Single

We gather together, it's a household feast.
Haven't seen each other in a while.
There's a new addition to the ones who call you auntie.
We share the same wrinkle around the eyes,
But I still know little about you.
One parent is the same between us two.
When it comes to conversations,
We've had less than a few.
Brother and sister in innocence,
We pulled the switch from a familiar tree;
Our path to grandmother's house rarely flowed differently;
Our feet became rough walking on the similar dirt road of our ancestry;
When did we become distant family?

Sitting in the pews at the back of the small Pentecostal church,
Not paying attention,
We were all close,
Despite the loss.
Before we had a cell phone,
We spoke every Sunday.
A reminiscent time, when our aunt was in the kitchen cooking up a big meal.
 Someone was braiding my hair too tight.
While others played hide, seek, and sometimes fight.
Our parents were raised siblings and when they didn't speak,
Neither did we.
Cousins that frolicked mischievously,
We pulled the switch from a familiar tree;
Our path to grandmother's house rarely flowed differently;
Our feet became rough walking on the similar dirt road of our ancestry;
When did we become distant family?

Our fingers sled through the wire fence after school.
Impatiently waiting for the moment when we could draw a connection on the side walk,
Throw rocks, and hop through it,
Hoping that all of life would be this easy.
Now age lines cover this face, it's been many seasons since we sat together in these church pews.
Someone dear took their last breath.
Grandma's house is long sold.
No grain of sand left to remind us of the path to that dirt road.
But we still share the same wrinkle around the eyes,
And wash our feet in the river our relatives once swim through to be free.
Even though it's been countless moons,
There's no way we could be distant family.

They watched those youngest while the parents were away.
Kids at the age of seeking someone to admire.
Sitters, the age of foolish mistakes and learning.
Each aunt and uncle had a follower,
A niece or nephew to call a favorite,
Until those smallest grew taller.
Now we commune through detached ends,
Barely meeting each other's side,
Only making contact when money is the need,
Or a favor is the request,
And the one asking expects that our connected blood will magnify generosity;
Making every response, yes.
In a moment of want distant is far from the tongue,
And it is family who are presumed to not shun.

In Love With Single

Prodigal

In Love With Single

I saw my sister aging quickly working in the sun;
So, I drove to a city not well known
And played the lottery for the first time.
Hoping to share the news I'd won.
Because when we were kids she pushed me on the swing.
I'm older but she experienced life before me.
I've moved in and out of her house
As the moon rules my sign.
Tripped and caught my fall an infinite amount;
Blind to the visible lines.
Discouraged at the end of it all,
I called the wrong person in a crisis,
'Cause I've relied on my sister too often
Expecting what's feasible,
And when she couldn't turn my water to wine,
I turned my back on her;
Not by way of questioning faith
But by taking an alternate route.
The result being, I went to someone who instead of carrying my stones,
Cast them at me.
I don't know if I can return to what was before
When it is I who ran away.
Yet, you still believed I'd reappear once more.
From a distance, again, I saw her aging in the sun;
So, I took on more hours,
Gained riches,
And then went back to aid her.
She tossed aside my offered wealth,
Greeted me with unfiltered loyalty and said,
"My fellow sister, let me be your shade
In hopes that you will never again be burned."

Simple

In Love With Single

In my many years
Nose in Bible
There are a few verses
Engraved on my tongue
Among others
One
Love your neighbor as you love yourself
Two
There is nothing new under the sun
So
Love whom you want to love
Love what you want to love
Just don't harm anyone in the process
Believe in the Divine
And
You'll meet the Supreme Entity above.

Some Still Sit

In Love With Single

It was another Sunday. I would usually attend with my mom and sister while dressed appropriately, sitting in the pews, and attentively listening to the preacher speak on the fear and judgment of God. He'd expressively voice this, in hopes of conveying the respect we should have for the Deity. During that same time, my dad and brother would typically be home comfortably watching whatever they want, while enjoying a woman free environment for a few hours. I'd be in denial if I said that there wasn't a hint of envy towards them being able to sleep pass the alarm. But I went expectant. I was present in church as an observer, witnessing the little flames react to words. I'd sit there willingly hearing but not necessarily listening. The message was too rehearsed. So, I remained distracted by my own thoughts and uncertainties. In the end, leaving my sit unmoved.

It was another Sunday but I was much older. I sat on hard wood, among other bodies, some pretending to have nothing needed from there church visit. In a place representing hope, we would anticipate guidance and inspiration to come from the mouth who is also, like us, imperfection. I waited for rawness to be spoken. I found it necessary to hear untampered frankness that day from the representation of empathy. Instead, the speech was recycled from the book of Job telling how he endured all. The words were lost of feeling. However, maybe that is the scripture a disciple refers to in moments of weakness. Then a pastor left the pulpit and all remained meaningless.

Again, much older, I presented myself seated for another Sunday. I was there for something new or reassurance in the habit I was tempted to lose. Desiring to be impacted enough to change my mind with words, silence the noise in my consciousness, and reach me in the pews. I sat not expecting to hear, but heard a sermon I could preach to myself during daily devotion. One making light of God's wrath and placing fear in the judgment. I then questioned my posture and recognized a repetition in myself, along with other flames, that never appeared to move. Completely focused on a messenger who carries the same mantle of imperfection along with myself and the ones I'm next to. This is not aimed to discredit the role a pastor and disciples have played towards reaching souls. Nonetheless, when disaster strikes, some still sit, while those struck ask, "Where are you and the one in whom you boast?"

Journalist:

Do you think someone could be a poet if they don't feel emotions strongly?

Author:

Yes. However, to be an impactful poet, I believe you must feel emotions deeply.

Good Poems

In Love With Single

Sometimes the most

Intellectually aspiring

Emotionally inspiring

Poems

Are either the shortest ones

Or the ones that carry on too long

Of such having first read

Seems empty of meaning

With an inconsistent iambic pentameter

And misused words

But strikes the core with substance

When what is written

Is pulled from the truth of feeling

Braces on Brokenness

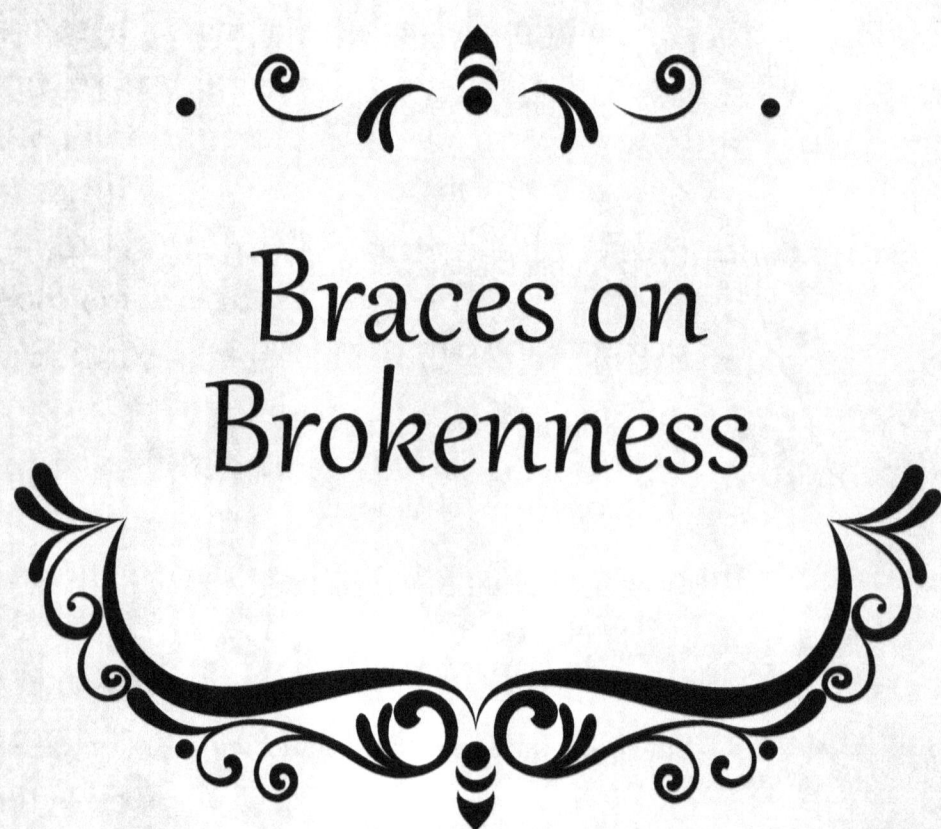

In Love With Single

You're afraid to say what's really on your mind
Make truth alive
So, you hold the heart by hand
Hesitant to extend
The torn pieces.

Instead, you aim to self-mend
Put a cast over what's broken
Straighten the bent bones
Fix your crooked smile
Alone.

Keep going
Find a cure that doesn't kill
Say you'll pray it all away
Then find the wound
Not healed.

Lay in your coffin without sharing pain
Remaining toughest on yourself
Concealing a mess that's never clean
Left buried
Leaving damage, the last seen.

Couldn't quite admit you panicked
Leaving the ruins exposed
You continued to rebuild alone
There are worse things than the blues in your skies
Others are far more damaged than realized.

So, place braces on the brokenness
Fix the crooked bones
A soul cannot be mended masked as stone
While risking more hurt, reveal your shattered heart as meek
Then be assured reaching out isn't weak.

Carry My Tears

In Love With Single

I'm sure you have better things to do
Than listen to my problems that are seemingly minuscule.
But I've reached the point of desperation
And I seek your therapy
Before hope reaches the point of non-existence
And the weight of my tears become too heavy to carry.

I'm the stranger,
That wears the smile and hides the bruises.
You caught me singing to myself on the drive to the highway.
I wore long sleeves that day so my husband's hand print was not visible.
He came home angry that night and left no room for me to share the news.
My breasts are cancer filled and crying too.
You kept looking at me
Throughout the time span of the red light.
Yeah, you saw the tears
That slid down pass my smile
But you couldn't tell if the cause was joy or sadness.
You just assumed
That the weight of my tears could not be any heavier than your own.

I'm the stranger holding that sign;
Feed me, donate to me, provide me a job, or like most
Simply look at me, then keep driving;
Because you assume I'm pretending
And I actually have a car in hiding and a home where I sleep.
If your vision were perfect then you would be able to discern
That the fraud you describe is actually the one begging across the street.
You kept staring, observing my worn clothes and shoes,

Then your eyes moved up to the words on the card board.
Yeah, I noticed your debate
Just as the light turned green
And you decided to keep your coins.
Chuckling and mouthing to yourself,
"His tears could not have been any heavier than my own."
I'm the stranger in that business attire.
My car is luxurious so you admire.
If you could see my heart,
The exposed version of me,
Then it would reveal the darkness that produced the gun hidden in my glove compartment
Meant to end my life of misery.
Still, you continue to admire and assume that my life is better than yours.
Yeah, I'm aware that you long for this image that I've worked so hard to create.
If you stare too long you may catch a glimpse of my passenger,
Self- hate.
It surprises me that you aren't observant enough to see the depression on my face.
Slow traffic allows you the opportunity to speak,
But you keep quiet, thinking,
"There's no way he'll respond to me."
"One look and he'll see my tears are too heavy."

I'm sure you have better things to do than listen to my problems.
After all, I'm just a stranger and my burdens are unfamiliar.
But in order to breathe hope,
I seek your therapy.
Carry the weight of my tears for just a second,
Then tell me if it's heavier than yours.

Ripples

In Love With Single

There is a sad shock when one makes a final leave.
All are unexpected, though some are prepared for,
But neither makes mourning absent.
While the eminence of farewell is known,
It becomes more real tomorrow,
When a presence I just spoke to, has departed;
Making it hard to determine who will stay and for how long.
There are many images that pass my eyes
But only few remain lengthy enough;
Leaving a trace before they're gone;
Causing ripples that keep me floating through currents;
While the small waves don't know it;
Their impact isn't visibly shown;
Often not even to me,
Until I start to sink when one bids me bye;
Then I'd see the imprint left behind,
Where the ripple touched my life;
Disposing remnants of how beautiful it is to exist;
And I'd wish upon all the stars
That the water beneath not keep still;
But continue to pass waves that leave traces;
In order to keep afloat,
Lifting me up to face the above;
Until it's my time to depart,
Drawing tears at farewell;
A sign that I was someone's ripple
Who left a mark before gone.

Great Again

In Love With Single

Is this the in between?
The Anti-Christ and then the end.
There's a president
Who promises to make America great again?
But I fail to recall when it was.
Could it be when the red, white, and blue forced natives to leave,
Or enslaved the ones with skin like me?
I can't say it's when segregation was at hand,
Because it never left.
The land divides rich from poor,
In certain areas color still separates,
With hate existing void of discrimination.
The red, white, and blue history never seemed great,
Just sustaining.
The elected leader wants to build a wall to further split
The line between freedom for all.
Proceed to bring it back to when women had no voice
And homosexuals couldn't get married in court.
To the years when a Tallahassee plantation couldn't be owned
By my grandfather, whose skin was dark.
Yet he tended his land through the strength of protest
And his river never dried.
Maybe that is the magnitude the elected describes?
Or could this be the in between?
Still every constant, I'm told
These are the last days.
But he promises to make red, white, and blue
Great again.
Possibly not the Ant-Christ.
Possibly not the end.

Trending

In Love With Single

This must be the photo causing all the buzz;

It's trending cause he's with her;

She's with him,

Got the guy in two days,

How?

Pay attention, it's worth the fuss.

Her body is plastic and getting all the love,

Gaining followers.

What did they do to lose all the weight?

Let me watch the video,

See what they ate,

On that diet of greens, vinegar, protein, and berries.

The hype begins with a popular voice that carries.

Create the hashtag,

Then witness the viewers echo;

Taking a stand for a cause that matters,

Black or all lives,

Can't forget women's rights,

Let me join in,

Mimic the publicity,

See how many likes I get,

March until my stance is fixed.

Times up for the artificial sentiments.

What's trending in this minute is shortly nonexistent,

With care shown until the buzz is no longer heard,

While promised actions remain resistant.

I Favored Kindness

In Love With Single

They'll always be a brighter day
Where the rain reflects shine
Making the grey appear lovely.
There are those times
To look towards the sky,
Elevate hope while down
On your knees at night.
Even after prayer seems vain,
When earthly angels fall
By way of cruelty
Leaving no power with kindness at all.

I favored chivalry.
Before one pulled over to offer a hitchhiker a lift
Only to lose their life.
Another rolled down the window to give
Only to be attacked.
At the same hour
Someone's daughter paid for a ride,
Was driven to an unfamiliar location,
And then raped inside.

I favored courtesy.
Before speaking wasn't about one's own feeling
But leaned more towards routine.
Politeness says Hello
But what gets returned is silence,
Attitude prior to words spoken,
Someone who won't hold the door open for the next person.

I favored being ready to help the weak,
Unbiased.
Before it was learned how to disguise
And one assumed feeble
Took advantage of the aid
Provided by way of those caring.
Before someone righteous went on a mission
Only to be captured and tortured
Leaving those at home hopeless.

I favored kindness
Before cruelty took away some of its power.
Now I proceed with caution,
Although at times seemingly vain,
Continuing to pray, even after.

It Happen to Whom

In Love With Single

I can't say it won't ever happen to me.
I go about surrounded by strangers,
Whom are the embodiments of weapons,
Moving in hopes that each human I pass is good.
I can't say I'm unaffected.
I walk around blinded by routine,
Until disrupted
With an unforeseen evil.
I remain aware of uncertainties.
I interact mindful of cruelties' presence;
How it occurs, where, and to whom continue to shock,
Yet, numb.
The gravity of a massacre weakens as it becomes the norm.
I still look towards mercy and ask to be overlooked.
I would be relieved,
If only inequity didn't maintain objectivity,
Then the death toll rises, beating the previous calamity.
There are tragedies.
God allows it,
Due to the permission of free will,
Pushing me to fear that there is no safety,
Making children terrifying to bear,
Causing a prayer.
Please, horror don't come close.
Prevent the events that leave one feeling spiritually forsaken,
Leading to the question,
How does evil decide whom to transpire against?
Faith is comforting sometimes,
Until I'm touched,
When it's too bad that all isn't good.
When I become the affected.

A Victim's Legend

In Love With Single

They made the news.
We know their history.
What caused them to step out in the devil's shoes,
Unload on those they don't know,
Avoid justice by turning the pitch fork on themselves,
The final act to their show.
We remember their faces,
Those demons who swore themselves right,
Boldly looking at the witnesses,
Proud of the scene that caused their tears over the now lost lives.
But we don't recall the victims.
Their images aren't in our memory.
The news failed to repeat why their breath had meaning.
The report just kept mentioning the perpetrators,
Painting their portrait,
Making them legendary.
While the casualties were quickly forgotten.
Unless the gone is a family member, friend, or someone who mattered;
The evil, a drug
The dead, an artist
Whose music or movies were great
But became best after the overdose
And the body laid to rest.
The news broadcasted the story.
The white had mental issues,
The brown was a terrorist,
The dark was a thug,
According to the report.
We learned more about the hand holding the weapon
And less about the massacred who fell while trying to run.
Their faces should be plastered in the history books our eyes see daily,
So that we don't forget the image,
Leaving remnants of the effect,
By remembering the victim's legend.

Not A Fan

In Love With Single

I knew it was always out there. The hate. But it wasn't always closely felt. Now with the advancement of technology there is no closing the eyes to it. Each image fuels the fire and every posted opinion on social media fuels it more. One is tempted to be mad, take up arms, and defend a label. This person was innocent, the one you labeled had no weapons present, and this individual's hands were up in surrender. Yet, because of another's fear and hate, there lays the image of a person who is now not breathing. By the hands of a human, another human is dead. Hate is humanity's worst capability, not listening to understand is its greatest weakness, and fear is its most misleading emotion.

I know it's not as bad as it once was. The racism and prejudices. People seem to be somewhat more accepting. But if I wear certain attire, adorn my hair a certain way, or if certain misconceptions about my particular race and ethnicity are believed; then the perception of me is altered. Acting upon an assumption about an individual or group of individuals is dangerous. One having the power to corrupt a pure seed. But maybe if we end the labels. Maybe if we silence the noise that causes us to act based upon false assumptions. Then the only images that would be viewed are those that fuel peace, equality, and love. Essentially, the perfect habitat. Since this will never be, it is safe to make this assumption of me; I am not humanity's biggest fan.

single

In Love With Single

adjective:
only one; not one of several; unmarried or not involved in a stable sexual relationship

synonyms:
one (only), sole, lone, solitary, by itself/oneself, unaccompanied, alone, unattached, free

noun:
an individual person or thing rather than part of a pair or a group.

In Love With Single

Journalist:
How did you come up with the idea for your current book?

Author:
The idea came when I grew weary of venting. Anyone who's been single for a long time knows just how aggravating the comments, questions, and dating scene can be. (Mockingly) Why are you single? You should do this or go there if you want to meet someone. Your standards are too high. You can't be picky. You're not going to find everything you want in a guy. There is no such thing as the perfect guy so don't wait around expecting one. Maybe you're seeking a guy who is out of your league. (Shrugging shoulders) The approach that I received from others gave way to the impression that to be single is a problem requiring a solution. I did not agree with this view. Therefore, I began to write. Then one poem lead to another, observations inspired narratives, and each manuscript drew towards a similar conclusion which encouraged the title of this book.

Hollow

In Love With Single

Her soul is walking hollow, in a trance;
Reflection no longer known.
He took pieces of her essence before he left
Leaving her heart abandoned.
She rings the sirens to awake,
Warning the ruins to return solid.
Because she couldn't escape what karma had in place.
She slept with a demon resembling her father;
Whom didn't know retribution would date his daughter,
And re-enact his foul escapades with women.
Had he cautioned her, she may have avoided emptiness.
Now she's fighting to walk on foundation again;
Only to build a path that lead her son to become someone like him;
Depositing wreckage with every affection;
Because his soul is walking hollow in a trance,
With a reflection no longer known.
He was exposed to a distorted heart that drained most of his core.
Having no guidance, he knew not of the sirens
And never returned solid.
Moving on to other bodies, passing the void.
He was a toxic king born to a mother who destroyed every guy that offered love.
She wasn't aware retribution would date her son.
But the spell blinds karma's actions.
They use to be the nice ones.
Now, they fellowship among those who are whole
Determined not to be uncovered as the hollowed
At least not until creating other shattered souls.

Connecting Parts

In Love With Single

Wear your heels, you're going out tonight.
There's a sense of liberty in the air.
Don't have to hide,
You'll be among your peers.
No stones will be cast at the reveal of your femininity.
He enjoys the scene with no worries of family in mixed with the crowd.
Who would condemn the life of she;
Whom walks boldly in heels;
Although born physically like the one who seeks to prove his masculinity.

Go dance with your friends.
Especially with the one whose husband;
Sits, while everyone stands,
And stares at his wife;
Who forced him to go out;
'Cause her friend is convinced of liberation in the air.
He watches them move freely.
Then his wife glances over,
Encouraging him to join,
But he detests the one dressed as she;
Whom he sleeps with that dances gracefully;
Although matching his physicality.
So, he doesn't budge from his seat,
Focused only on the one he married.

You're feeling glamorous and notice your friend's husband looking displeased;
Arms crossed, not smiling,
Trying hard to prove his masculinity;
When just last night you both meant nude,
Connecting your identical parts.
With no witnesses you participated in intercourse.
Unashamed, the one with the ring, confessed an attraction.
The admission left you unbound;
Leading to this night you wear your heels;
Knowing he won't reveal, yet hoping he'd at least give
A hint of appeal towards you, unsuspectingly to his wife;
Whom has faith that her man embodies all the qualities associated with testosterone,
But his manhood is reliant upon a shield that repeals the free will of identity;
A future that hurts both dancing parties
By way of convincing heterosexuality.

That Day

In Love With Single

Coming up on that special day

And she viewed it bitterly;

Watching folks reserve their spot at restaurants

Weeks in advance,

Hearts everywhere,

Pink and red in demand.

She's reminded of what's lost.

It's just another day,

She'd voiced,

Ain't nothing special about it.

At her request people walked on pass,

None said happy,

Then she'd dismissively compliment their rose deliveries.

Leading to that night an acquaintance provided an update.

The one whom affected her bitter just weeks prior,

Got broken up with.

Then showing a picture of the two,

She looked at the reason he left her blue,

And found the replacement to be beneath she.

The information received

Made that Valentine's day satisfactory.

Perfect Apron

In Love With Single

With a little caffeine,
Her apron remains unstained,
Walking in the kitchen, two toddlers tide around each leg,
Carrying plates of food recently made by her hands.
She has yet to rest since the conclusion of work,
But she doesn't complain with reason of what her body expresses.
Provided one hand, she iron's the clothes for the ring,
With the other she prepares school lunches for the sperms it gave.
Her voice manages their homework and gets them ready for bed.
At night she's expected to be okay with keeping the apron on untattered.
At sunrise, she holds the coffee, careful not to spill,
As she gathers the kids for their routine morning trip.
The display is empty,
Slipping out before any eyes opened,
Leaving her with a load.
But she's alright,
As she says goodbye to the children.
Apron tossed to the side,
For a few hours she could contemplate about her discontent
With that protective garment.
Before sunset she picks up the small ones,
Genuinely ecstatic to see them.
Typically, prior to reaching home,
The ring is already comfortably in its display.
But this time it was vacant,
With the exception of a letter.
In spite of her tidy apron,
He chose not to stay.
With an unpresented sense of relief,
Looking towards a bright horizon,
She wasn't the one who committed the act in this family environment.
It was the ring who pretended to be alright,
Even though it was him who demanded the perfect house wife.

I Observed a Wife

In Love With Single

I observing a wife
As she wears the bracelet given on an anniversary.
Standing in front of the mirror taking too long to get ready.
She handles herself with care
It's date night
Which has become rare.
When everything is prepared,
She anxiously waits for him,
Only to receive a phone call while sitting in the dining room.
He's working late tonight.
Cancel the plans, they'll reschedule.
She pretends everything is alright,
But she can't hide the mourning behind the fog.
He promised her always
But committed a time.
Vowed their love long lasting
But lied.
She had plenty of time to think while he was away.
It was the first I noticed broken tears.
I observed that wife again the next day,
While folding his laundry,
Her eyes secretly searching for clues,
Answers to her suspicions.
The husband walked in greeting her with a seemingly unforgotten passion.
Though it appeared her mind was prepping for the scene of them fighting
A dream she had while falling asleep in an empty house
Not disrupted until she heard him creeping in the late hour
And lying next to her, backs faced to each other.
The space between them resembling neglect getting colder.
Although it wasn't literal,
She shared her thoughts with me.
Images of a doomed marriage.
Behind the walls were the arguments that I would never see.
A bad investment whose reward is only a lesson.
She pulled back, looking in to his eyes for signs that are genuine,
All the while battling her heart at every truth spoken.
Either he's faithfully committed or she's crazy enough to bleach his clothes.
Still in her mind's space,
she recognized her passion for their love
As a one-sided addiction.
Months later, I observed a wife separated,
And sharing a cautionary tale of her union.

The Silence Meaning Thru

In Love With Single

"You're suspiciously silent," is all I could say. There was a whole conversation replaying over and over again in my mind of things yet said. Typically, I'm the quiet one in the presence of another. Gravitating towards those who speak in abundance and don't find my response of few words discomforting. So, in that extended moment where neither his voice was heard nor an enthused expression shown, I grew concerned.

"I have nothing more to say," was his only response during our drive back home from dinner. We had the worst kind of argument, the one that doesn't end with passionate love making. It had been building up for months. He was doing too little and I wasn't doing enough. There were no raised voices or items thrown. Our tone was calm, nonetheless, he remained on one opposite end and I the other, while we ate our meal. At lose of fight and last bite, we stood, both leaving the table unsatisfied.

From my experience, the most vital conversations happen during car rides. Possibly because the drive symbolizes the turning point that determines a destination. We drove that night but the vocal exchange was nothing said. Staring into the skyline, I realized the infinity in words. There are countless ways you could use them to express factors that are reoccurring. One word with a specific definition could have so many translations depending on how it's said. As we drove that night, each passing car represented something unspoken. That quiet expression formed a conversation of clarity. Subsequently, our ride was over when we parked at what use to be our home. Leading this woman of limited utterance to break the stillness and say what we already knew. "You should pack your bags. I think we're thru."

Repeat Break

In Love With Single

I entered a home newly single. My eyes took in a space that hadn't been felt in over a year. I breathed in the extra drawers and room in the closet. I accepted that the indent which took shape from his body on one side of the bed would no longer feel his warmth. I didn't sense an ounce of longing until I noticed the walls were empty. Not one hint of his presence remained. Then the thought I'd been trying to avoid, came; maybe he'll return to me.

The next day, I prepared a list of things to do; join a gym, get my revenge body, and move on to someone new. Getting over him should be easy. I read an article that mentioned the signs of withdrawal after a breakup: depression, irritability, fatigue, and loneliness. In the nights to come I felt every symptom. Waking up in longing. Providing a facade at times with the mask of a smile. I knew it would take a while to recover.

After all, there are different kinds of heartache in the same way there are of love. I can't say one heartache is greater than the other. The intensity is dependent upon the person who handles it. Having the same conclusion; the person you are at the beginning, you aren't at the end. I began to reorganize my space and fill the void. Then with slight changes, having even used an alternate approach, I moved on to the next experience hoping to avoid a repeat break.

Let's Try This Again

In Love With Single

"Mm, let's see. Tinder, P.O.F., OK Cupid, Zoosk, Match, or E Harmony?" There were so many online dating sites to choose from. However, meeting someone, with whom I share a common attraction towards and a common status of availability, at a social event seems less than likely these days. So, I attempted to connect other ways. Sill I questioned if I would miss what online dating is lacking; the opportunity to observe a potential interest in real time prior to approaching. Despite reluctance I moved forward in a search speared by the fear of ending up alone. Holding on to the thought that Kings and Queens aren't fashioned on a bed of solitude, I continued to fiercely launch a pursuit.

Potential: "So, what do you like to do for fun?"
My thought: Swipe right on Tinder and see who responds.
My reply: "Hang out with friends or just chill at home and enjoy a Netflix binge."
Potential: "Why are you single?"
My thought: Cause the pool of available men in my area suck.
My reply: "I just haven't had much luck as of late."
Potential: "What would you say is your best feature?"
My thought: These questions are boring.
My reply: "My smile. You?"
Potential: "My arms. Would you like to meet?"
My thought: I guess I'll give this online dating thing a real shot.
My reply: "Sure."

I waited at Starbucks, while pretending to read, anxiously watching for him. I saw this guy approaching with a limp. His face looked altered, stomach appeared to be a few inches larger, and I could've have sworn his profile said he was taller. The potential that could've been, never informed me of his true image. I forced myself through the evening.

Potential: "Can I see you again?"
My thought: You lied.

My reply: "Maybe but I see us only becoming friends."

With my phone in hand, I continued to swipe. Engaging in mimicking conversations. Meeting bodies with no agreeable connection or appeal. Until another.

Potential: "Hi"

My thought: Here we go to answering the same questions again.

My reply: "Hey"

Potential: "So what was different about your day in comparison to your last?"

My thought: Oh, that's new.

My reply: "I got up out of bed after the first alarm whether than the third."

Potential: "LoL. Not to sound abrupt but I'd prefer to talk to you in person. Can we meet?"

I arrived at Starbucks, the potential was already there, appearing as the truth of his profile. I approached, effortlessly completing the evening, and forgetting the time as we spoke.

Potential: "I'm glad you're single."

My thought: Ditto

My reply: "Ditto."

Then midnight came with a text.

Potential: "Babe, I'm horny. Can I come through?"

My thought: Well that didn't last long

My reply: "Hell, no. Too soon."

I placed my phone down. In weariness, I deleted all online dating accounts, took a hiatus, then returned; in hopes that the online scene would have a new supply. When the product remained the same, I decided to put my phone completely away, and forget the search. While worrying not if I'd find that heart which attaches to mine, I fashioned myself in to a Queen by way of solo.

In Love With Single

In Love With Single

Journalist:

Let's briefly discuss your journey, thus far, as a single woman. What has been your relationship experience? How long have you been single? Do you hide any secrets, such as your successes or failures as it relates to relationships, in the book that only a few people will find?

Author:

The only secret not plainly detailed in the book is that of identity. Only a few people will know of whom a poem refers or if it refers to anyone in particular at all. I'm a pretty private person. With the exception of a few friends, I don't make a practice of discussing my relationships or lack thereof with people. For the reason, I find there to be no point to engaging in a conversation that will voice opinions which are repetitive or non-beneficial. However, out of pure excitement for this book, I will share openness, and state that I have never been in a serious relationship. The longest I've ever dated or spoken to someone was for a few months. To add, those few months didn't always carry consistent contact. (Shaking head and chuckling) Nonetheless, I don't place any fault in my character nor do I fault men for this outcome. This is just the course my life has taken and I am steadily unashamed of what's destined. I have found that when attempting to push the hand of fate, I am unsuccessful and conclude mentally drained. Therefore, I don't force relationships of any kind, but rather allow them to happen or not, naturally. With that being said, I've been single and celibate for years at a time.

As If

In Love With Single

Imagine me

Your reality

He gives

All to her

Screaming more

Lays it hard

She can't

He won't

Let the

Connection go

Passion with risk

Commitment with jealousy

Pulling envy

Through the screen

My shipping parodies

Cry when

they breakup

Pushing for

A reconciliation

As if I

Were the one

Part of the couple

Instead of she

Imagine me

With the man

On TV

Someone Already Has You

In Love With Single

We meant at a bar,
The play-offs were in charge.
You sent glances my way,
I felt the flame,
Returned a smile.
The familiar story of courtship.
Until weeks later he explains.
Despite, I continue to nibble on his forbidden.
With heavy guilt, I enjoyed his experienced lips.
I wanted to find someone available
And thought he was it,
But part-time company was all he could offer.
I tried to be accepting because I liked him that much.
So, I continued.
I'm a loner at heart,
Finding silence at times comforting.
However, when being alone became too much,
I called at your closed hours
And you turned me down.
Asking for forgiveness during your next open minutes.
Somehow convincing me to stay.
Become that one hidden
Until he is ready.
You tempted me by saying you'd leave
And I fed in to the dream.
Never inviting you between my sheets.
That action would cause me to lose all dignity.
When the alluring appeal drew me close to loss,
The sympathy for a wife's tears wouldn't leave my heart.
So, I shut the door and turned the locks.
In spite of your efforts,
I didn't see you again,
Until a random visit at a grocery store,
She was with him.
I walked right pass like I would any other couple of strangers,
As if not noticing, without a voiced message.
The short dream was tantalizing.
I was almost hypnotized.
But once I snapped out of it,
Removed the gloss from my eyes,
There was no convincing me otherwise,
I'm not one who could stay hidden,
Simply accept and be the side chick,
All while,
You're committed to someone else.

90's Babe

Twist My Hair

In Love With Single

He may be drawn to the years he has yet to see.
I may be drawn to the youthful tightness of his body and energy,
At any rate, we can't help staring with excited arousal.
He's always ready.
I'm always ready.
At twenty past midnight he messages me.
At four minutes past thirty I respond admiring.
The glory of age.
I grew up in the 90's,
While he was still a babe,
But that didn't stop him,
But I didn't make the catch easy,
Kept stringing him along,
Still, he continued to claim me.
I provided no obligation to his wrong.
With each encounter,
He showed me what authentic stamina feels like.
With each encounter,
I showed him no commitment and that enticed.
So, he sought to prove that nine years in between isn't reason enough.
And in doing so,
He made me lose all reservations.

In Love With Single

Walking on unfamiliar waters;
His skin is the color of ocean sand,
Mine, the black grit of Iceland.
The mixture excites my senses.
We proudly walk in public,
Showing our shade of hands intertwined.
Some glance at us from the side of their lazy eye.
If I could, I'd take a picture of the stares
From those lenses that divide.
As a couple we moved forward.
Our minds open wide to the possibilities,
Disregarding the stereotypical differences.
He loves Country and a little Hip Hop.
Learned to groove to my Rhythm and Blues.
At dinner he eats sushi.
I despise it,
While my mouth chews on chicken,
On my plate,
 A side of pigeon peas and rice.
We share the same drink that we're both use to.
Then at night, we shower.
He slides right in under the sheets.
I follow, doing the same,
Only to pause and twist my hair.
Those like my 4c know it's a must before bed
To avoid waking up with a nappy head.
He observed me, tilting his face
As if witnessing something strange.
I thought, "if he could not grow to understand
And love my hair,
This part of my Rhythm and Blues,
Then it's over,
And I've discovered a problem
With dating outside my race."
He finally spoke,
"Your arms must be tired,
Let me help you twist the back
So that you can put on that satin scarf
And relax."

Mind Song

In Love With Single

He played each key with the correct finger
His every note echoed my vocals
My lips moved to his freely provided melody
While my hips swayed to the music of seduction;
The lyrics read
Intimacy while fully clothed;
His ear remained in tuned with little effort
Matching me
Rhythm to word;
Then we went home separately;
My mind song;
I want him to know all the pages of my story;
So, I dived in harmony;
He sexed my soul
Teased my flesh
Then left my core void of his filling;
Claiming abstinence until marriage;
My mind song;
He skipped the page that read
My patience wanes when my body is frustrated.

Pump 9

In Love With Single

I'm feeling kind of off today,
Ready to snap at the next person who sends imprecise words my way,
I may need space to gain some clarity.
Just then, he spoke sensually
A true language that offered the remedy.
The end result will calm you and make people more tolerable,
He assured.
You are feeling uneasy and a bit restless,
So, I won't be gentle with this method.
Sit on me, spread wide, move up, down, and then circle around
Using your fastest motion.
Break me.
But don't you grow weary in the act,
He admonished,
This route to destress is lengthy
'Cause I'm taking you to pump nine.
Position yourself in to a wheel
While I work my way in,
Next relax and rest your legs on my arms,
Let my tongue massage.
This moist action will have you walking with a smile all day
Thinking about the ways we laid.

I have anxieties,
Is what I confessed to him,
As each pulsing move eased tension.
It is why I don't favor depending on anyone.
But for this need, I relied on him to satisfy,
Expecting to reach a promised level.
He glided around the walls and then tormented the tip,
Gaining encouragement at the sound of my moans.
He went in, rough,
Forgetting the world at the command.
I embraced the force
Until the weakness could no longer be avoided.
I exhaled the agitation.
The stream cascaded in to oblivion
While he lay pleased with the results.
Knowing his words were true,
I closed my eyes completely unwound,
Gloating in the sensation of reaching pump nine.

Heard Nothing

In Love With Single

I thought he would've called.
So, I called him and got no answer.
Would I get a call back or a text containing an excuse?
Instead, I heard nothing.
To avoid obsessive pondering
I filled my mind with distractions.
Perhaps in midst of an activity
My phone would ring or a text from him may appear.
A week past and I heard nothing.
Then my phone vibrated with his words,
"Hey, I'm sorry. I've been busy."
He waited.
Expecting a response.
But instead,
He heard nothing.

Triggers

In Love With Single

Here I go.
Reacting to the same old words.
I should've stood there unharmed.
Pretend it didn't touch any fragile nerve.
But instead I yelled every defense.
Called the truth a lie,
Because I heard it too many times.
So here I go.
Removing myself from the situation.
Putting distance between those who truly love.
Pulling away from what recalled the damage.
Because in anger you spoke out loud,
Breathing life to my triggers.
So here I go.
I provided warnings early on.
Henceforth, you knew,
Just what bullets to release,
Held the gun and aimed it perfectly.
Maybe you thought I grew,
Past what provokes during the time you knew,
And didn't expect any backlash;
Since when I walked you ran behind,
Tried to rebandage each wound,
Lessen the mechanism it ensued,
But your attempts weren't a success.
So here I go.
Reacting to the same old words.
I know I'll soon return,
But because I can't quickly erase
That you used my triggers
To shut your case,
 I resort to tendencies by withdrawing.

Confidently Insecure

In Love With Single

Going about, doing the ordinary

Purchasing groceries, caught stuck in a long line

He's looking at me, while with her

She notices the exchange, then assumes that I want her man

Yet, I don't agree with the attraction

He's prone to sneaking around, you're threatened by female strangers acting

confidently insecure while with him

I have no desire for what you've acquired, less envy for the glare found humorous

Continuing on about, I greet him who is not my attraction

Sparked appeal through provided information, we walk the strip a dozen times

Discussing possibilities, my gut rings doubts

He speaks of a picture I don't own, my presence becomes a ghost

Could've wanted him equally, had not my body been disobedient

We move forward on about, through shopping centers passing many

At one, he waits in line

While holding an item, a female stranger approach

Thought to be distracted, I notice the exchange

Had not we'd been dating, of her he seems intrigued

I was prone to speak, carelessness wouldn't agree

I went on about, astonishingly enough wanting to encourage the chase

Providing him more space to talk with her, I left confidently insecure we have a future.

One-sided View

In Love With Single

My lover seems so far away;
Standing as I lay;
He claims we tried;
And said it without meeting my eyes;
When I reached out he pulled his hand;
Staring out the window to a view;
Miles from our actuality;
While I don't have much experience with relationships;
I am aware of the work it takes for them to grow;
I realize once you stop all efforts to of me discover;
This change, however significant, didn't threaten my world;
I'm an expert at being on my own;
Still, I'm too fond of you to loosen my grip;
Placing stubbornness aside;
I overlook his reluctance to try;
By taking steps to move closer.
When one has shut a door that isn't transparent enough to walk through;
It's challenging to exhaust all attempts to fight resistance and prove;
Things could be easier;
Had not one given up the effort and the other allowed the grip to weaken;
Desire would be vulnerable to know both sides of longing.
In a different space it was I staring out the window;
Wishing I didn't have to put forth so much effort
Just to hold a lover in my arms;
Who slips in without force;
With whom understands and consumes me;
However, the courtship when not smooth;
Leaves one looking upon a mundane view.

No X's

In Love With Single

He saw me trying to hide,
Came at me bold,
Even though he knew the odds were
 I wouldn't be interested;
And still he thought to give me a try,
But why, when I had my eye on some other guys.

Introducing one, who tossed my champagne to the side,
He preferred wine,
Told me I wasn't an option,
 Called me delusional for thinking I'd be his first choice,
Then he left with no remorse,
Took me by surprise,
All the lies I told myself,
Like give him time.

So, I approached the next confident with my best line,
Said I'd eat his smile,
Gave him my number,
Was upfront with what I wanted,
And a few sun's later he was gone,
Either he was too weak or
 I came off too strong.

Then there's the one with whom I was reluctant to converse,
But allowed him to come close,
The infatuation snuck on me,
I revealed the feels, let him dip in,
And then he became a ghost;

Alisia Latoi

Assumed me needy, I suppose;
Now there are no X's to know.

For this scene, I went by courting rules,
Not appearing desperate,
I teased enough to encourage pursuit;
Although I wanted him more,
I acted as if I cared the least,
It worked for a period,
Until he pulled back,
Then I dropped the mask,
Showed him great affection,
But he didn't last,
Still leaving no X's to know.

Back to the kind I hid from in the start;
While adhering to dumb advice,
I spoke to him despite my lack of interest,
But couldn't force appeal for long,
Subsequently, I bid him bye,
Calling him like others,
No X's to know.

Provided the flow of what life offers,
I've only had those I use to talk to,
They'd come, they'd go;
Those I wanted to stay, would turn and leave;
Yet I'm still a victorious being,
Seen as the one with problems.

In Love With Single

Purchased Vibration

In Love With Single

Hey purchased love,
You've impressed me tonight.
I can't deny the need
When his body isn't in reach.
You made yourself available
Always ready, fully charged, and able.
I close my eyes to let my imagination and hands take control,
Put you in,
Then seal you away like I'm ashamed,
But that's not the case.
I would wear you proudly and gloat in my night
Of self-satisfaction with your aid,
But it's a bit taboo,
So, I'll just lay here with a grin,
Giving freedom to the sensation.
Sex is great.
Without a partner,
It's a dream,
Made somewhat real,
With my purchased vibration.

content

In Love With Single

adjective: in a state of peaceful happiness.

synonyms: contented, satisfied, pleased, gratified, fulfilled, happy, cheerful, glad; unworried, untroubled, at ease, at peace, tranquil, serene

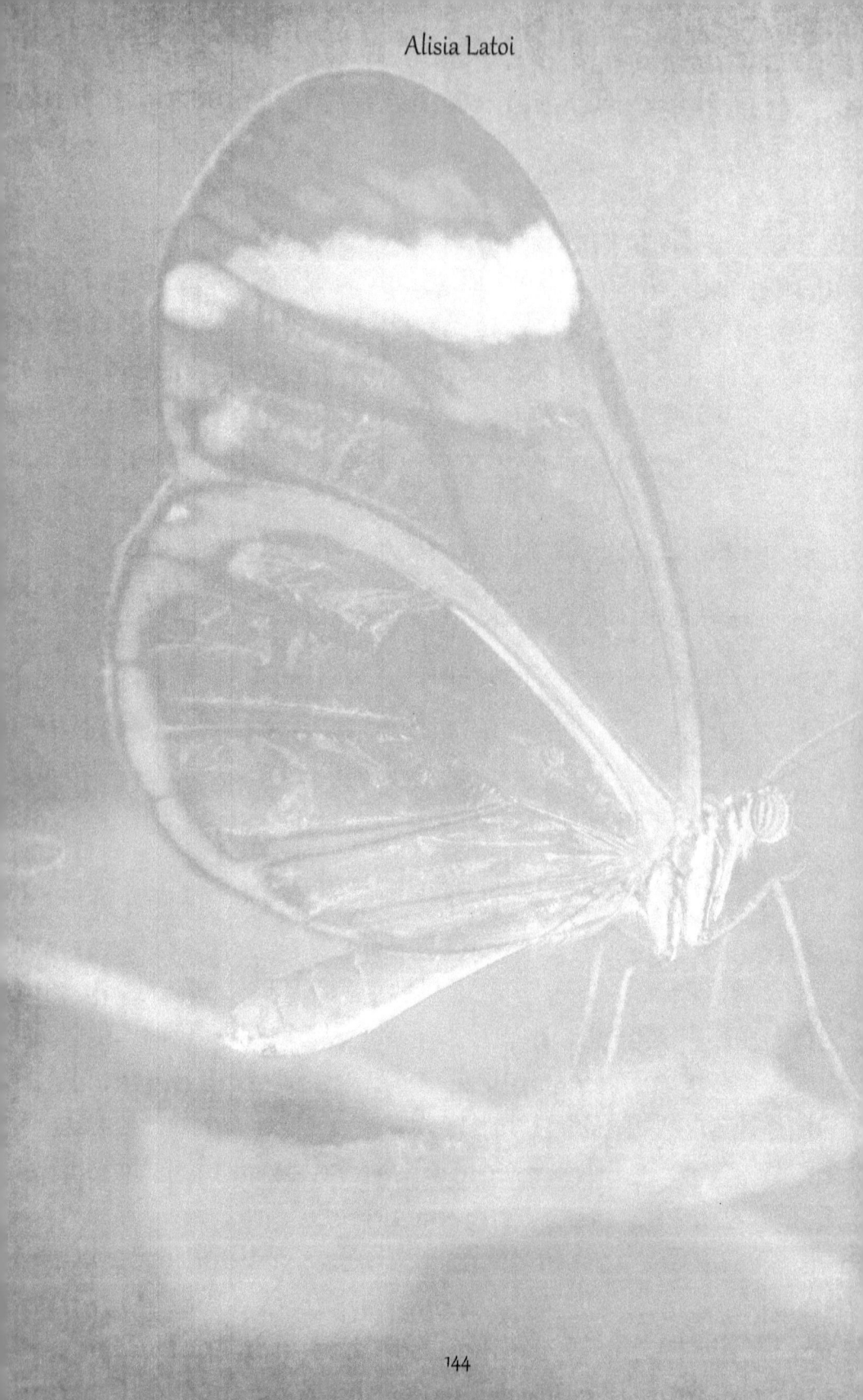

Alisia Latoi

In Love With Single

Journalist:
What is the main thing you want readers to take away from your book?

Author:
I wish I had something insightful to impart into the readers, provide them with tips to live by while single. The main thing I want them to understand after reading the book is that the topic at hand doesn't just refer to the lack of a significant other. It's about embracing your unique status while in a state of contentment. I don't have the resolve within myself to follow through a union in which my soul fights against. So, I gained an acceptance of and learned to be okay with the possibility that marriage or that type of long lasting commitment might not be fated. Yet, I'm living a life that I adore and all other particulars are owed no explanation. Single is the current that I am at peace with. (Smiling) If my perspective alters, it'll be in the next book.

Without A Pair

In Love With Single

Find my most attractive picture,
Post it online,
And type in the description my best qualities.
While I don't believe they'll be a positive outcome;
It's just another way to demonstrate my availability.
After all, I'm without a pair.
With the passing of time,
Doubt moves in and crowds my space,
Convincing me no one is out there.
Do I really want to repeat the same conversation with another potential match?
Tell him a little about myself
To discover by the end of the evening
His key doesn't fit my lock.
Couldn't possibly be a moon for every planet.
No way of stumbling across my missing sock.
Becoming numb to the idea of meeting my counterpart.
Should I continue the search
And repeat similar events of meeting men
Who at first interaction ask to lift up my skirt.
Then there are those that continue to boast about their accomplishments
Leaving no room for you to discuss yourself.
While the others lie online and spill the truth when they greet your face.
The worst to come across,
He has a wife and needs an escape.
Then the cycle continues as I mix and mingle.
Because I'm without a pair.
Missing a sock.
Becoming numb to the idea of meeting my counterpart.

For Three Words

In Love With Single

My walls were built on a foundation of neglect
But I tore them down
For you.
Spilled the clues that left me open
Gifted my heart without wrapping
Placed outside of the box
And you received it.
I expected a return of great value.
Instead got imitated jewels
That rusted with little tampering
Leaving me with the conclusion,
If I can't have the desired equivalent
Then there is no reason for giving vulnerability
To the possibility of three words containing eight letters
That will create new walls having a foundation of misuse.

Be Direct

In Love With Single

It's pathetic to stand there guessing;

Cease the hints and desist leaving mixed letters;

Replace candor with the scrabble game;

Be precise with what you mean;

If it's not within my desire;

I'll speak the truth to you;

But have the courage to see my nakedness;

As I cleanse my exposed rejection;

Cover the scars left from the past;

And understand the impact caused by the history it fed me.

When you look at my open wounds,

My mind may be lost to you.

Still, be direct with your words and I'll offer the same courtesy

By explaining every misunderstood moment with honesty;

Because it would be wretched to stop at a closed end

Without attempting to revive communication's life.

So, be candid with care if you fear strife.

We may conclude on opposite spectrums,

But at least both on the side of truth,

Bringing vividness to our words,

Eliminating suspicion,

Directness removes.

Single Status?

In Love With Single

I object the way you misinterpret my single status,
Stepping on it with your idealism and time constraints,
While you assume my life is lacking.
You pin me down,
Waiting for the day I have a significant other to complain about in your presence.
Forcing your opinions in my ear;
Go out, step up, flirt more;
Attempting to crush my individuality;
Yet my wing's not damaged.
But you keep asking me my age, what's my status,
Constantly pointing out your opinions as to why you don't see a ring;
Reminding me how I've been single since we've first meant,
And asking me what's the excuse;
Because I should be married or at least in a relationship by now,
From your point of view.
Yet, I'm here, asleep in the middle of a king size bed,
Unashamed to lay by myself with unshaved legs.
I live risky cause I'm a few paychecks away
From calling my car a home,
But I survive self-reliant.
Witnessing someone who lives otherwise
Leaves me unaffected.
Unconcerned with the idea of spending the rest of my days independently,
I walk rejoicing.
It seems no matter how happy my single reality,
I'll be perceived as the women standing alone.

Never Lowered

In Love With Single

I won't go in to details about the quality guy I am attracted to
And describe what's handsome to my eyes.
When it comes to magnetisms, the specifics are not important.
However, there are certain characteristics and principles that entice me.
Some of which, I will not deviate from expecting,
With having no lenient appeal in relation to firm subjects, such as belief and politics;
My circumstances will never alter them.
Yet, there are few exceptions to this rule.
Nonetheless, these qualities are not impossible to meet.
I encounter them in men often,
Falling short in the chemistry of connecting personalities.
I am quick to argue against the accusation,
Having standards does not dissuade a potential relationship.
There is no fault in wanting one's own particulars.
With having not compromised the values that are important to me,
A woman who has been single for a long time
Bears no need to lower their standards in hopes of meeting the one called settling.

Amends to Body

In Love With Single

From hair strands
To toe nails
I picked
And dissected
Held high criticisms
Unsteady esteem.
I ripped apart
Covered flaws
Compared attractive
To others' drawn.
I battered
Left little accepted
Torn separate
Was this skin.
Until withered criminal
I plead guilty
To the offense.
Of trespassing
Punching shame
Vacating the scene
Witnessed unconscious
The flesh was me.
Clinging to life
Short of breath
Robbing all lovely
Confessed a thief.
Of stealing beauty
Truthful uniqueness
Wishing different
Original shattered
Suspect to victim
Returned humbly.
Admitting not wrong
Strokes painted right
Held in contrast
Self-caused pain.
Owing apologies
Dislike laid to rest
To this body
I make amends.

In Love with Single

In Love With Single

Hello, my name is Anonymous. I am an individual but society labels me, single, and I accept it. However, not by the definition the word implies. I once had the words desperately seeking a relationship plastered on my forehead. It was printed in bold ink on my online dating profile, on my attire and body language during outings with friends, and easily noticeable during conversations with strangers. I lost myself in the search for a lasting relationship. Each attempt and ending failure stirred up the irrational idea that there was something wrong with me. In seeking, I became blind to the treasures of my surroundings. My only observation during the search was that I appeared to be without.

Then there were the outside voices. For a time, my single label was accepted and not questioned by society. The more time I spent with the label, the more observers viewed me an anomaly. Subsequently, after passing the common age of marriage, concerns were more frequently spoken from the outside voices. The common belief that it is not good for a human to be alone, encouraged the observers of me to question and advise. Why are you not with someone? In my individuality, there is faith, and this faith reminds me that although the tangible appearance seems to be by one's self, I am never truly alone.

I managed to silence all other noise. This individual now stands, viewing the reflection of what is tangible and listening to the inside voice that feeds the soul. A soul that was once bruised in its attempts to change a label has become renewed with a different purpose. My new search is focused on maintaining and expanding my joy in life. This type of joy that I seek is never ending happiness. A happiness that lingers during times of sadness. Marriage may come or it may not. My version of single is not fearful of being by one's self. In seeking and holding on to all that I rejoice upon, I find no space for the desperation that leads to non-fulfillment. An outside voice may question if I am looking for a significant other. My response is no. I only seek joy. It would be great if another is a part of that kind of happiness, but if one is not, then my joy will still be great.

I, Anonymous, make this vow, to protect and honor the soul which abides in this temple. I promise to uplift and nourish this soul by limiting its exposure to that which is poisonous. Single does not equate to loneliness or lacking a relationship. It does, however, imply that my primary relation is with self. While open to the possibility of having a relationship with another individual, I stand, viewing me, in love with single.

In Love With Single

Journalist:
Very well said. This interview was a pleasure and I look forward to what's succeeding.

With that, I graciously shook Ms. Fields hand before she bid her farewell. Free of the thoughts that presented itself prior to, I washed the glasses and returned my living room back to its original design. Once all was in place, I called my confidant to update her on the flow of this evening occurrence. Preceding the overview, she asked the pivotal and initial enquiry same as the journalist, replacing the present with the past tense. "Were you...?" Drifting off on that last word, I filled in the blank before it was uttered. When presented with authenticity, readiness is never questioned. However, when lacking, the uncertainty of preparation is always there. Giving the circumstance only what is true existed. So, I responded, "Yes, I was." Having expressed the enlightenment of my infatuation with being single, I intend to remain prepared for the likelihood it continues. In which case, I endeavor to not be discouraged.

Follow Alisia Latoi on Social Media.

FACEBOOK: "Books by Alisia Latoi"

www.Facebook.com/alisialatoi/

INSTAGRAM: @author.alisia.latoi.books

Alisia Latoi can also be reached via email:

alisialatoi@gmail.com.

Author's Bio

Born and raised in South Florida, Alisia Latoi received a Bachelor's in English and Sociology at Florida Atlantic University.

Writing poetry since the age of nine, her poetry style is free form and Alisia's first collection features poems written in her early years, adolescents, and young adulthood.

www.ingramcontent.com/pod-product-compliance
Lightning Source LLC
Chambersburg PA
CBHW020139130526
44591CB00030B/147